E-COMMERCE END OF THE YEAR RUSH-SALE STRATEGY

THE EXACT BLUE-PRINT TO TRIPLE YOUR E-COMMERCE STORE ON BLACK FRIDAY, CYBER MONDAY AND CHRISTMAS!

DAVID NELSON

On Dec 29, My Mentor Bob Will Be Showing You the 3 Step Formula to A 7 Figure Email Marketing Business and How He was Able to Generate 7 Figure with Email Marketing

You will Also Learn How to increase your e-Commerce sales using this strategy

Join the Awaiting List Now

http://7figure.launchrock.com

reviews and certain other noncommercial uses permitted by copyright law.

Note; At the end of this book, you will be able to learn the exact strategy to outsmart your competitor and make the most money in every end of the year

Thank you for buying

Advanced E-commerce End of the Year Rush-Sale Strategy

Furthermore, End of the year is when the most money is earned online, all you need is to master the strategy outline in this book to make the most money, outsmart your competitor and own an e-commerce store that will change your life!!

TABLE OF CONTENTS

INTRODUCTION

Anyone who is into e-commerce business already knows that anytime from September through to December being the end of the year it's always a hot period of time to make massive sales and money because people are always in the mood to purchase more item than ever before

It is a period of time where people mainly purchase products for their loved ones, friends, and family both at home and abroad.

Due to this I was inspired to write this book to guide everyone who is into e-commerce business to help them to run a successful online store to better increase their sales with the right marketing strategy and plan for every end of the year because I have spent years to acquire this knowledge and I know a lot of people can't afford hundred and thousands of dollar to purchase courses that will put them at the top notch to run a better marketing promotion for their product at every end of the year including **cyber Monday and black Friday** that everybody in the world is waiting for to purchase an item.

The strategy outlined in this book is a detailed strategy that both beginners, intermediary and advanced e-commerce marketer could definitely use to make a massive amount of money, generate a lot of product sales and get a lot of data that will make their facebook pixel to fire.

It doesn't mean whether you are new or old in e-commerce or which platform you used to create your store. If you are new you should get this book to compete with the top store in your niche and outsmart them and if you have been around for a while must get this book to transform your business and make your brand stand out from your competitor.

For this book, I will be using Shopify (https://goo.gl/t883bb). If you are just getting started you should START YOUR 14 DAY TRIAL NOW – (https://goo.gl/t883bb) to create your store in order to follow the step in this book.

You definitely need to be prepared for the upcoming best period of the year (**Cyber Monday and Black Friday**) to make a massive amount of money from your online store

This time is the major time every e-commerce (dropshipper) marketer dream of because of the special event that is coming up.

Even if you haven't made any money online before, end of the year is always a game changer to make your first $$$$ online and take your business to the next level if you play it well.

Get ready to discover what every e-com guru will charge you anywhere from $999 to $3000 before they could review it to you almost completely free today

WHY YOU SHOULD READ THIS BOOK

If you're desperately in starting and growing an online business or if you have been thinking of having a business that could pay far better than your present 9 to 5 job and give you control over your life, all you need to do is to follow the strategy to start and grow your online business.

This is an advanced e-commerce training booklet and will not take you through creating your online store from the crash. If you are just getting started and want to know the best way to create a profitable dropshipping business check out my previous book (dropshipping goldmine) and learn the right way to create a profitable online store

I have made it my mission to show every e-commerce owner the right way to run a successful online store and generate anywhere from $1000 to $10,000. Once you make your first one thousand dollars, making your next $100,000 is just a step away because you can reinvest the money earned to make more money

End of the year is always the best time to make a huge amount of money because a lot of people will be purchasing an item as ever before

This book will be the vehicle to help every e-commerce owner to run a better end of the year promotion to make either their first thousand dollars or take their store to the next level.

This is an advanced e-commerce training so now I will let go to chapter one to know what e-commerce agenda really mean

Happy learning and I so much believe you will get a lot of value in this booklet that will transform your business

Chapter 1. E-commerce Agenda – The Foundation

First of all, most people ask this question; is free + shipping still work, what is the best way to run a retail promotion and is there another option to free + shipping?

To clear your doubt, free + shipping work extremely well if you do it perfectly and run a lot of targeted traffic to the product page. Another thing is the description. You need to write a description that is perfectly ok like creating urgency and scarcity in the product description e.g. **hurry only a few left in stock; we are giving this product to X number people for the next X hour, we sell out fast; you will never see this product in any store. If it's a Print on Demand product you can say something like this; this is a custom printed from our company and you will never find it elsewhere e.t.c**

There are series of ways you could do this above is just an example to give you an idea of what am trying to point out. Including those word in your description increase sale over %100 and make every visitor stack their cart with a lot of product.

Free + shipping does make your store generate a lot of traffic that will fire up your Facebook pixel to better reach a big audience of similar people who have an interest in that your product. Beside Facebook have the data to prove that

Retail product mostly don't work well when running advert and the reason is that people you are marketing a product of $20 to $80+ item will hardly purchase from you because they haven't seen your store before though they like the product but they will hardly spend that amount of money with you because they have not purchased either receive an item from you before, in other words, they don't have enough proof to trust your company to deliver that product to them and that will make them go to the bigger brand like Amazon and eBay to purchase similar item that looks exactly like yours.

To answer the third question, the other option to free + shipping model is the retail promotion method but there is a strategy behind this which you will discover below

What you need to do is to first create that reputation to your customer and the new visitor to your store before advertising more expensive item to them and that will lead you to master **email marketing** for e-commerce because through email marketing you can advertise more expensive item to your existing customer. Later in the feature, I will be writing a guide that will show you how to run email marketing for your e-commerce store

What I will like to elaborate is that there is a better way to first run your first retail product promotion which will make you better than your competitor stand out from retail promotion. also work better than free + shipping model but the major thing is to try both systems to know which really work better for you.

FREE + SHIPPING VS RETAIL PRODUCT PROMOTION

Below, you will know the better way to do this and be above your competitor

The science behind this two system is very powerful in sending a lot of people to your store and makes your brand look very trustworthy. All you need to is master it well and you will thank me later

Below you will discover a very powerful and useful strategy to run both retail product promotion and free + shipping model

FREE + SHIPPING (F+S) PROMOTION STRATEGY

Like I said earlier, free + shipping work extremely well but the major reason why people fail with free + shipping is because they market the wrong product at the wrong time meaning they promote a product that does not have a sizzling effect e.g. product that is not trending which will lead to losing money during advertisement and also lead people saying free + shipping doesn't work anymore

Sizzling means something that is trending at a particular time at a stated time

To run a successful free + shipping promotion and avoid losing money on advertisement, we need a product with sizzle effect

HOW TO GET A PRODUCT WITH SIZZLE EFFECT

To get a product that has sizzle effect, we need to make use of a tool created by Google. To get started go to trends.google.com and see what is trending right now

Another thing you could do with google trend is to input your niche keyword in the search terms and see if the search volume is above %50 but if its below don't go for it you can check my previous book dropshipping goldmine to learn how google trend work but for this strategy, once you are on the website navigate to what is trending right now and see what if people are searching for on google. If you find any trending term, all you need to do is to find the similar product you can promote to that audience from aliexpress or print on demand (POD).

Pricing F+S Product

Once you have identified what is trending from google trend and find a product that is suitable for that particular trend, what you need to do next is uploading that product to your Shopify store or any platform you are using and prepare to run promotion with either facebook ads or any other traffic source you want to use but for this step I will suggest you use Facebook ads and start your promotion from anywhere from $20 above since it end of the year and you want to make sure you compete with your competitor out there but if its not end of the year you can start with $5 ads and scale up if the ads are profitable. You can also you this strategy for either the beginning of the year depending on when you find this book. The thing is it works any time of the year but mainly meant for the end of the year.

You want to price your F+S product anywhere from $9.95 to $11.95 or you can even drop the price to $8.95 depending that you still profit from every sale you make. This is a business and no one wants to lose money by all miss. You want to this to be a win-win scenario. If you find a product from aliexpress or a POD at anywhere from $0.99 to $5 you are still good to go with the $8.95 through to $11.95 F+S model

F+S are meant to do one single thing and that is the major reason you need to consider running a free + shipping. The major goal of F+S is that it quickly

- ➢ Blitz facebook fan page
- ➢ Blitz facebook pixel
- ➢ Blitz email list
- ➢ Blitz social proof

When you are able to blitz your fan page, email list, social proof and facebook pixel your business will keep ascending and you will gain more customers but If its retail promotion you will get less traffic, less sale, less comment (social proof), less email list and facebook will not fire as expected by doing so, you are not blitzing anything and you will not get the result you are expected to get.

Though not everyone will respond to the F+S (you cannot please everybody) product because most people will think that's not through, they will assume they're not getting anything for free since they are paying to ship for the product while some will be so excited to claim their free product and pay for shipping. Due to this, you need to carry out the second method which is the retail promotion strategy

By using the retail promotion strategy below, you will realize the power behind the strategy and discover how you can destroy people objection in purchasing an item from you

RETAIL PRODUCT PROMOTION STRATEGY

The retail product promotion strategy happens to be a cool way to replicate the same result as the F+S strategy but notes that we are not running a promotion for an item that is $15 above. We still want to get the same result as the F+S strategy.

To use this strategy the right way, we still need a product that has sizzle (might be aliexpress or print on demand product) effect with a

- $5 retail price +
- $ 4.95 shipping price per item

The psychology behind this is that someone who sees the F+S price at $9.95 and did not purchase the product might see the Retail price at $5 and purchase the same item

Note that, they still pay $9.95 for the retail price because at checkout they will be charged $4.95 which will now equal to the same price as F+S

To make this work better you going to use a hot keyword for your image design e.g.

- Flash Sale
- Steal
- Clearance

See image example below

$5

$5 FLASH SALE TODAY ONLY

$5

80% OFF CLEARANCE TODAY ONLY!

80% OFF CLEARANCE TODAY ONLY!

The image example I use above is a print on demand example. The one with the currency sign is an example from the print on Demand Company. What the company does is that they allow you to add your design (maximum 4) to pillow and promote it to your customer.

The power behind the pillow is that you can make a customer to spend more money on your store from just visiting your store for the very first time

See the example of the dog paw pillow above. A customer will not purchase just one pillow but will be tempted to purchase the four-phase pillow that spell love. One more thing is that the customer will end up spending more money on our store. Meaning, instead of spending $9.95 for a single product he will end up spending almost $40 at a single order.

Note, this company charge $5 for their pillow and the $4.95 charged for shipping is definitely your own profit. Above is just an example you can do this for aliexpress. Assume you find an aliexpress bracelet for $3, $5 or $6 you can also do flash sale deal for the product. All you need to do is to copy the exact image ad in the picture above.

The **flash sale** word is what I love using and its what top marketer in the space uses because it send a signal to the shopper that they won't last long and it happen right now. This simply create urgency for the customer and make them purchase the item instantly.

Using this method, we still achieve the same result as the free + shipping mode. That is, we still have the opportunity to blitz our

> ➢ Email list
> ➢ Fanpage
> ➢ Facebook pixel
> ➢ Social proof

And next thing I want you to know is by doing this we are getting volume for our store and blitz as well

Don't also forget that you can split test both promotion strategy at once. That is, running the F+S and the Flash Sale to the same audience at the same time and the best thing is to run the ad at the same time and watch which convert better for you.

What you also need to know is that when running this type of promotion, we will be getting a lot of traffic to our store which will lead to

- Building an email list
- Having a lot of abandon cart
- Facebook pixel firing
- Have tons of facebook fan page like

This is what we need to take our store brand to the next level and by getting all this data, what we do next is to ascend our business by sending more expensive similar product ($12 $24 $40 $55 $65 $ 70 $ 100 $125 e.t.c) to our customer through email marketing. I believe you now see the possibility of building a real business fast here. From selling low ticket product to get the customer to buy high ticket item (upsell) which is mainly called the back end money.

HOW TO MAKE EVERY VISITOR PURCHASE MORE THAN ONE PRODUCT

As explained above with the pillow strategy, you can make every visitor who visited your store to make more than one purchase at the same time

Any visitors who see this archery pillow will not only purchase one pillow but rather get the whole set of the pillow.

The science behind this strategy is making every single visitor spend more money with us on their first visit to our store. By so doing, we find out our customer will fall in love with our store and will always love to buy more product from us when they receive their first product.

You can apply this step to any product not only pillow method. Just think outside the box and see a design that will allow you to sell more than two or more product at a go

CHAPTER 2. FACEBOOK FAN PAGE STRATEGY

Facebook fan page is regarded as a business page. Most people don't spend time on their fan page to reply to comment in other to increase their engagement. Whether you are getting a comment or on your Facebook ads or the post you made on Facebook, there are some comments you must respond and there are some comments you must get rid off in other or it not to kill your conversion and lower your brand loyalty and brand.

In this chapter, I will be showing you some cool strategy you need to know and some kind of comment you must respond to on both Facebook fan page and Instagram. Presently Facebook has a lot of feature e.g. going life on Facebook, advertise for free, create an event and offer e.t.c. though the most types of this feature are always profitable if you have a lot of highly engaging fans.

This strategy will drastically help you to improve your organic reach (free traffic).

FACEBOOK FAN PAGE BENEFIT

There are some cool benefit facebook has that will help you improve your organic reach. The most important thing you need to do is to engage with your audience because your facebook fan page is known to be a community. Once you are getting a lot of engagement then you can make use of some of the cool feature (benefit) that Facebook had. Some of those cool benefits are

> Comment engagement – always respond to comment both negative (or get rid of it) and positive comment
> Offer claim
> Facebook lives – it's not must to be on camera to go live on Facebook
> Facebook custom audience
> Facebook messenger engagement

Once you have everything going on perfectly you want to really make use of the feature to improve your engagement and get organic reach on Facebook. Another thing you need to do with your fan page is post regularly e.g. assume you have a cat store and you create a cat facebook fan page, all you need to do is post several cat image, articles, youtube video, gif, and funny memes to improve your fan page engagement which are

- Shares
- Likes
- Tags
- Comment

Once you start getting this kind of engagement coming in then your facebook post will start to reach a lot of audiences and get massive exposure

RULE OF FANPAGE

For your fan page to get organic reach you need to abide by this rule below

1. Post lot of content on your fan page
2. Engage with the audience: when you engage with your audience. Facebook will start seeing your fan page as an active community that provides value and in return of this facebook will credit you by giving your post a massive (free traffic) exposure.

There are some question you can do without replying to and if you don't reply to those messages, people will see your page not active and might make you lose customer trust. On your fan page, you want to reply to

a) Pricing question
b) Variant question – color, size, and type
c) Sales question

With conversion question like

a) I like this
b) I want this
c) I love this
d) I need this

This kind of comment is conversion comment. People who made such comment love the product but might not want to purchase by the time they saw the ads. In other us to trigger them, what we need to do is to reply to them back with a discount price. The comment should look like something like this "**hey, thanks for commenting on our page, for taking your time to comment, here is a %% OFF we created personally for you**". Now when a customer sees this kind of reply to their comment, they will go to your website to purchase your product because of the discount you offer them.

This will make customer love your brand and will make them want to share your brand with their friend.

You also want to reply or delete conversion killer comment

   a) Rip off
   b) Shipping takes time
   c) Pricing is too high
   d) I hate this
   e) Never received mine

This kind of comment are regarded are conversion killer or negative killer. If your customer, follower and those who find your ad see this kind of comment, they will not buy anything from you and that ad engagement will start dropping down because of the negative comment. What you have to this kind of comment is to **get rid of it as fast as possible or you can do something like replying to some of this comment by message them e.g. NEVER RECEIVE MINE – we are deeply sorry that you never receive your product by now, please kindly forward us the detail of the item you purchase from us and we will find your item and send it over to you.**

What happens when people see this kind of your reply it boosts conversion and makes customer trust you. If you can't handle this, you can hire VIRTUAL ASSISTANCE to do all this for you. It will only cost you some buck.

FACEBOOK CUSTOM AUDIENCE FOR YOUR FAN PAGE

Another hack for your fan page is to create a custom audience. For example, create a custom audience for all your

> ➤ Fans
> ➤ Saved post
> ➤ Message your page
> ➤ Engaged post

These are four group of different audience you can create a custom audience to retarget them. The reason for this section is that you can respond to every comment on your fan page even your virtual assistance will still miss out some comment. This happens because no one is perfect so creating custom audience will help you reach those set of people you or your VA can't reach through comment.

In summary, the strategy behind this is to engage with your audience and post multiple contents on your fan page every single day

Chapter 3. Black Friday & Cyber Monday Bootcamp

Black Friday and Cyber Monday are the best time of the year to generate a massive amount of sales for your product and make a huge amount of money at the backend. Think about it, last year alone there is over $3b transaction in just a single day. What signal does that send to you? I so much believe Black Friday and Cyber Monday are a game changer for anyone into the e-commerce business.

If you are a novice or a beginner, this is the right time for you to jump into e-commerce, create your store and play around with marketing. Also this period of the year it will be the right time to make your first $$$$$ online if you haven't made any before because over the period of this time there will be a buying frenzy that is almost everybody will be purchasing an item online even locally so it a very big opportunity to get started. If you are already into the space and already have a top-selling item in your store, this the right time to take your store to the next level and generate a massive amount of money. You don't want to afford to miss out on this buying frenzy that will be happening on every end (black Friday and Cyber Monday) of the year and if you miss out, I bet you will regret it because this is one of the easiest opportunities to get started with e-commerce and play the game well and crush it

The information I will be sharing with you on this chapter is very powerful and no one teaches this for free instead you will be charged hundreds or even thousands of dollar to acquire this single skills.

Since this happens to be a great event of every year, you need to be prepared ahead the time in other to catch up. The reason is that a lot of (your competitor) marketer are also looking to blast out this special day.

STEP TO BLACK FRIDAY & CYBER MONDAY

- ➢ Be prepared
- ➢ Create a Black Friday Collection
- ➢ Master Black Friday Discount
- ➢ Focus on top selling product
- ➢ Create black Friday facebook ads
- ➢ Email marketing

BE PREPARED

For the black Friday deal, you need to be prepared. What am trying to say here is that you need to be fully prepared because you are expecting to flood your store with traffic which will definitely equal to sales and also you want to make sure you keep every of your customer happy by making sure they receive their product on time. In respect of that, you need to talk to your

1. Vendor

Contact your vendor (they need to be prepared for scaling) and inform them what you are about to do. Let them know you are about to triple or quadruple the number of sales you are getting before and ask them if they can handle the shipping

2. Virtual assistance (VA)

Your virtual assistance needs to be prepared for customer feedback because you are going to be getting a lot of customers sending in messages concerning the product they order or want to know more about your business. So your virtual assistance needs to be prepared to answer questions

Quick tips; always have customer mindset to avoid having a negative comment and to take your business to the next level

CREATE BLACK FRIDAY COLLECTION

You definitely need your store to stand out from every other store by adding this little different. What you are expected to do here is that you need to create another **product collection page** on your menu bar **named "Black Friday Sale",** take note; once you created this page a month or few weeks to black Friday or Cyber Monday, don't add any product until 12:00 am on Black Friday day.

The power behind this is that every visitor who visited your store will be opportune to know that Black Friday is coming up and they need to come back on that day to claim their special discount. Since they are already your customer e.g. they have once purchase from you, you will reach them through email marketing.

I want you to take note that every visitor who visited your store every end of the year are always looking for black Friday deal on your menu bar because they know it is a special time to have the special discount from you. So I believe you now agree with me that it is a very brilliant idea to have the black Friday collection available before that day

To create black Friday menu bar see the SHOPIFY image below

Once it black Friday day, what you will do is to add the best buy product from your store to the black Friday collection page, you can do so by following the number 3 in the picture above

MASTER BLACK FRIDAY DISCOUNT

Another thing to take note is that you want to master a black Friday discount. The reason behind giving a huge discount is that customer already knows that they are meant to get a huge discount during black Friday promotion since that what black Friday is meant for. But the question here is that how many discounts should you give to your customer on Black Friday? All because it a black Friday shouldn't mean that you should lose money. To avoid losing money in giving out huge discount you need to know your

1) Your number

You need to know how much discount you want to give away that will not make you lose any money e.g. you are not advised to give away %50 to %75 off on a $30 to $80 item when you know that you will lose money but if you make money with it you are good to go. The major thing here is that you should know your number before setting up your discount for your product

2) Discount strategy

As we all know that %10 off to %25 off is always a regular discount during the year, so you don't want to give away that kind of percentage off on that day. Good black Friday discount should start from %40 through to %75 off. First thing is to know your number and conclude which one will be suitable for you. I will suggest you don't play with the %75 off because you might end up losing money if you don't do the math perfectly. %40 to 50% will be extremely ok. E.g. Giving away %50 off for a $50 item that cost $15 to purchase night be very okay because we still profit about $10 which is cool. After giving away your discount rate and still profit about $5 above, you are on a better deal and if you are getting more order that shows that you will definitely make more money from the $5 profit margin. First thing is to know your number (profit margin) to know which discount will be suitable for each of your product

3) Increase some product price

Assume you want to do some discount for some item that cost about $10 on your store and you know you will lose money giving away %40 to %50 off what you could do is to raise the price of the product to $20 to $30 during black Friday and create your discount price for that product

4) Keep shipping in mind

With the shipping method, you can still make most of the money you are giving away back. Assume an item on your store cost $18 and you apply the %50 off discount price, mathematically we know we are left with $9 but now if we charge $4.95 for shipping we ended up making $13.95 instead of making $9 only. Always keep the shipping in mind because it might help you offer a better discount rate to your customer and also make more money back from the one you are giving out as a discount.

Note; you still want to have free shipping item on your store. Don't charge shipping for every product in your store

5) Create safeguard

You need to keep this at the top of your mind when you are creating any discount either on Black Friday or anytime. The reason is that most people lose money after creating their %50 discount. Here is how it happens, assume you want to create a %50 discount code for one or two product, instead of that code to apply on just that two product it ended up applying on multiple products on your store which will definitely lead to you losing more money on your side. Come to think about it, assume you only want to apply the %50 discount code on a $50 product and unknowingly to you that the code you only created for $50 product will automatically be available to a $5 to $10 product which will make you lose massive money at the back end and make you end up with $0 profit and that's what you want to avoid totally in respect to that you want to create a guard for any of your discount rate you are offering.

See the picture below

THE GUARD

Pay attentively to the picture above. What this tries to tell us is that we can make a customer to spend some certain amount of money before they can get the %50 off. What this strategy does is that it helps in increasing cart order. Customer will keep ordering more products until they reach $100 before they will be eligible for the %50 discount rate though that is not necessary. What am trying to point out here is the section I check with the red mark, that is the exact area you want to select the specific product you want the discount rate (%40 to 50% or lesser) to have effect on.

FOCUS ON TOP SELLING PRODUCT

For the Black Friday period, what you need to do is identify your top-selling product and focus on marketing on marketing them. You don't really have the time to start testing which product will convert better for you. If only two to three products are performing better for you, what you have to do is market those two or three products alone during black Friday. If you are just getting started quickly look what your competitor is selling through Facebook by entering some search time into facebook search bar e.g.

GET YOURS NOW + NICHE OR PRODUCT NAME

GOO.GL + NICHE OR PRODUCT NAME

FREE SHIPPING + NICHE OR PRODUCT NAME e.t.c

Find what is working for other and duplicate what they are doing

CREATE BLACK FRIDAY FACEBOOK ADS

Another thing you need to focus on is to create a special image or video ads for the Black Friday promotion. You want everyone who sees your ad to know that they are seeing a black Friday promotion deal by doing all you need to do is to create a **facebook custom** audience for your

- %75 video view to hit the best audience fast
- Past buyer
- Set all retargeting audience

EMAIL MARKETING

Email marketing will let you tell your present customer about your black Friday deal. You definitely need to take this seriously because this is where you will be able to tell your customer about the black Friday deal that will be coming up

For the email marketing, you will be sending out an email almost twice a day. That is from Friday, Saturday, Sunday, and Monday. On Friday being black Friday you want to send a promotional email two times that day. That is, 8 am and 6 pm through to Cyber Monday.

Here is what you need to do before black Friday

You want to send out a mail on Wednesday and Thursday to let your existing customer know about the Black Friday deal

See image example below

Now your customer will be able to see the email you sent to them regarding the black Friday deal. They will not be able to

order the product until black Friday but the only thing they will do is to pre-order (add to cart) the product.

- ✓ On Wednesday, you want to send out an email to your entire list about the black Friday deal while

- ✓ On Thursday 8:00 am, you want to send out another email to those who did not open your Wednesday email while on Thursday night at 11.00pm you want to send out a buying frenzy email to your entire list again to purchase their item. By that time you should activate your discount for the customer to purchase their item

Now after sending those email, now on Friday being black Friday you want to send out three different aggressive email to your entire list. Your first, second and third email should go out by

- ➢ 6:00 am – announce your %% discount. All product
- ➢ 7:00 pm – send out what is trending on your store with a countdown timer. Don't forget to include urgency like only 6 hours left to claim your item
- ➢ 11:00 pm – hurry, only one hour left to claim your %% off. Here is what you should do, send people to the collection, best seller and catalog product in your email

On Saturday, you want to email those that did not open your email on Friday, not the entire list. Let them know that they are having the last chance to claim their item

Before Cyber Monday, meaning on Sunday, you want to send out a mail by 11:00 pm to your entire list concerning the cyber Monday.

Note, you should do something different from the black Friday e.g. on black Friday you offer a retail discount code so on Cyber Monday you don't want to do the same.

What you are going to do on Cyber Monday is to do **FREE + SHIPPING AND $5 FLASH SALE DEAL**

On Cyber Monday you want to send out two email at

- ➢ 6:00 am
- ➢ 11:00 pm – one hour left to claim your special deal for Cyber Monday. Just make sure there is urgency in the email you are sending out and on your product description

When sending those email to your subscriber make sure you are sending out trending product and let them know that you are sending them the hot (what is trending) product to purchase at either F+S or $5 flash sale deal

On Tuesday you can send out another email to the non opener and let them know they are having the last chance to claim their free item.

That's all about what you need to do about Black Friday and Cyber Monday to make a massive amount of sales. All you need to do is to send out a mail at the right time. Remember, you are not the only one doing this, your competitor are also doing the same thing you are doing so you need to be smart and send out a mail at the right time and I believe you already got a training that your competitor doesn't have so best luck and go crush it

CHAPTER 4. MASS CONVERSION TESTING

Mass conversion testing is simply the ability to test the different product on a single page to know which product convert better. On your Shopify store, you can have up to three or four different pages with different niche e.g. cat, dog and tortoise page. On each page, you want to have 5, 6 or 7 different product for each niche. Below is an example

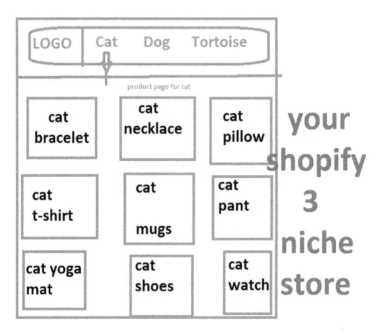

Can you see the power here? The secret behind this is the ability for every visitor to your site to see more than one product and being able to purchase more than one product once they landed on your store. The reason they will purchase more product is that they are the same cat product.

To get product for each niche you should use both aliexpress and print on demand product and your retail product price should be $10 to $50. Check different retailing store to know how they are pricing their product

Before you can generate a lot of sales with the strategy you need to market each niche e.g. cat product to a cat lover, dog product to dog lover and tortoise product to tortoise lover.

ADVERTISING STRATEGY FOR MASS CONVERSION TESTING.

Once you have this page set up correctly, the next thing to start doing is promoting your product through Facebook and Instagram. You don't really need to start spending lot of money on advertising, your Facebook marketing budget should be at $5 dollar per day while your Instagram marketing should be anywhere from $15 to $50 for 12 or 24 hours. Note, you are using Instagram influencer. To learn how Instagram influencer works, check out my book dropshipping goldmine. In chapter 9, you will discover how to start Instagram influencer marketing with a low budget, how to contact influencer and pricing

FACEBOOK AND INSTAGRAM PROMOTION STRATEGY

When setting up your Facebook campaign, you want to optimize for your ad for **PURCHASE** and either create a video you chose the carousol ad not a single image at this time. What carousol ad does is that it allows you to use more than one image in one single ad. For each niche, you want to upload all the image of your product so when customer sees your ad, they can see all the product you are selling at once. The power behind this customer who sees your ad might like the first product and will never like other while other might like the first, second, third and fifth product e.t.c

Don't also forget to only choose news feed display during your ad creation.

For the Instagram influencer strategy, you can download the facebook video or create a new video for this step. Just make sure there are combinations of more than one product e.t.c

Once everything is set up and running you will start getting lot of product sales and discover sizzle product. Conversion rate might decrease but average order value (AOV) will increase because each of your visitors will stack their cart and purchase as many of your product at once.

Quick tips; make sure most of your product are high demand thought it doesn't matter but always very good since the goal is not to have a bunch of product on the store. So the product should be converting product.

In the next chapter, you will discover the exact strategy that will help you make a lot of sales and generate a huge amount of profit at every end of the year

CHAPTER 5. RUSH-SALE STRATEGY

End of the year is really a special time in every year to drastically increase your income and blown out your sales. The strategy that will be discussed in this chapter is always applicable every end of the year, that is from December down to January. This strategy has nothing to do with the Black Friday and Cyber Monday but always the best time to make a lot of money at every end of the year. Whether you are a newbie or member doesn't matter here all you need to do is to follow the strategy in this chapter to explode your sales and huge profit this December.

Note, this strategy is only applicable every end of the year and its main purpose is to help you generate a lot of sales and help you build a trusted brand that will keep making sales during the beginning of the year to the end of the year. Even if you haven't made your first cent with e-commerce, you can use the strategy in this chapter to make your first $$$$$ online and keep running e-commerce business for the entire year. You will be surprised how this chapter will improve your business.

TOOLS TO USE

In other to scale our sales up, there are some tools that will help us to achieve that goal. The tools we need are

➢ Facebook fan page
➢ Email marketing

➢ Facebook ads – there are a couple of things we need to do here, we will retargeting those who VIEW CONTENT, ADD PRODUCT TO CART AUDIENCE and THOSE WHO ALREADY BUY PRODUCT FROM US.

The people we will be remarketing to at the end of the year will be those who already have seen our product before and who already know who you are. To get this done you want to drop your price down e.g. you can either create another collection or rename your black Friday collection to 35% OFF SALE and 50% OFF SALE COLLECTION PAGE. Make sure you have those two collections. Not must to do 50% off, you know your number so you should how much to give way that will not affect you. Once you create your collection, make sure you only add a product you can afford to give that percentage away.

After you have all of the page setups, you need to start driving traffic to that collection. The first step to take in driving traffic to those collections is to email marketing.

END OF THE YEAR EMAIL MARKETING

You want to start sending out an email to your list a week before Christmas. Assume Christmas is on Tuesday, you want to send out your first email on

• Thursday by 8:00 am. Your email subject line should be the END OF THE YEAR (%%) OFF SALES

- Second email on Saturday by 10:00 AM – same subject line
- On Tuesday being Christmas day you also want to send out another email at 10:00 am – subject line; Christmas day blow out with the deal (%%) you re giving out
- You also want to send out another email on Thursday (9:00 am) and Saturday (1:00 pm) of that same Christmas week
- On Monday by 8:00 am, you want to send out another with some urgency subject line LAST CHANCE TO CLAIM YOUR %% OFF.

Once you hit first day of the new month, you want to close all those stuff you are giving out because if you don't do that, your customer will not trust you anymore

The second thing you should do after the email marketing is the fan page strategy

FAN PAGE STRATEGY

The only thing you need to do is to keep posting every day (a week before Christmas) on your fan page. Your Image size should be 1200 x 1200 with multiple products with your call to action in the image 50% off sale

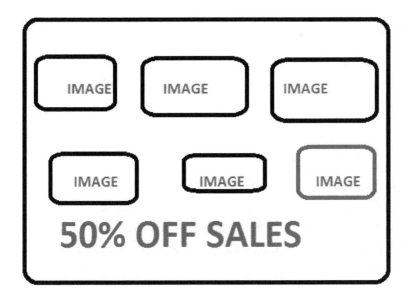

Link the images to the exact collection in your store.

The next step you should be taking after the email promotion and facebook fan page post is facebook ads

END OF THE YEAR FACEBOOK ADS STRATEGY

Step three which is the final step you should be taking happens to be the most vital part out of the two above. If you are new to the e-commerce, don't have a list, never build a fan page before, take a good part in the black Friday and Cyber Monday or you have been running an e-commerce store. The strategy is applicable to any person who is running an online store.

For the facebook ads, you will be running three different campaigns which are

1. **Cold prospect:** this are people who never seen your product before and during this ad campaign, they will be opportune to see your end of the year sales.

You want to create a new Facebook ad from the beginner and choose your audience through keyword e.g. dog lover, dog, mum e.t.c after which you will have to create a lookalike audience to expand your reach and increase your rate of success. Your budget for this ad set should be **$5 per day**

Note; you need the same image you are posting on your facebook fan page. The only difference is that this one is going to be a paid ads

2. **Non buyer (visitor):** this should be the second paid ad you should be running. This group of people who have seen your ad before and have never made any purchase from you.

This set of people have visited your website once "view content" and most of them who visited your store have added one or more of your product to cart "add to cart". These kinds of prospect are regarded to be a high converting audience and are likely to purchase if they see your ad again. Due to this, we will be setting up another Facebook ad entirely to target this group of people. Both view cart and add to cart are titled CUSTOM AUDIENCE. So for this ad-set, we will be setting up a custom audience to target this group of people

Your budget for this particular ad set should be **$10 or $15 per day.** The reason for spending that amount of money per day is because those group of people are warmer audience meaning they already know you because they have seen your ad before and visited your website. Another reason for this is because there is a limited time (two weeks) to run this ad. At the beginning of the year which is January 1, the ad must be turned off and the deal you are offering must be canceled

3. **Purchase audience:** These are the previous audience who have already purchased your item before so they are known to be the most profitable audience. All you need to do is to set up another custom audience to remarket to this group of people

Don't forget to use an image with multiple products with an urgency caption just as shown on the image above. Your budget for this kind of ad should be **$20 to $25 per day.** The purchase audiences are more likely to buy more product because they know us, they trust us because they already purchase from us and they are a happy customer.

The strategy discussed here is so epic and powerful. If applied when you will see your Shopify store or online store chat scale up instead of it decreasing. Every single step taught in this chapter are proven and meant to generate sales and make you a massive amount of money.

CHAPTER 6. $100K SCALING PLAN

There are a different and various strategy to scale your Facebook campaign to $100k and out of that different strategy, I will show you one of the specific strategies that is proven to work as a gangbuster. To scale your Facebook campaign to $100k, you only need to master one single strategy and if you can master the step I will be revealing to you in this chapter, you can scale your Facebook campaign to generate $100k in sales. Scaling your campaign to $100k does require a lot of investment. Don't expect you are going to spend $5k or $10k to make over $100k. With $24k to $50k with a proven strategy, you can scale a campaign to $100k to $160k if you implement the strategy taught in this chapter. Always know that you can start small then scale gradually till you reach that goal when you will be able to invest $20k to $50k to make six figures in sales with facebook marketing.

Before you think of scaling your campaign, there are couples of thing you need to take note. The things you need to take note are

> ➢ Your facebook ROAS (return on ads spent) need to be anywhere from %100 to 400% anything below 100% ROAS is not good for this strategy.

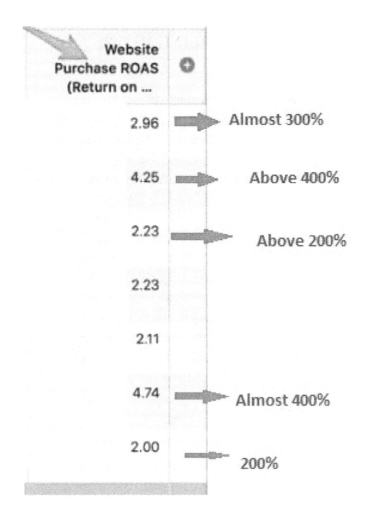

The picture above is how your ROAS should look like. Always make sure you have this kind of ROAS before you even think of scaling your ads with this strategy. If you are having this kind of roas that shows that you are having a lot of engagement on your ads and you are getting a lot of view in your store. The next thing is to scale your campaign to the next level

➢ You want to make sure your ads is a video ads. And you already got 1k above video watched

Now that all this is set up and you are getting a lot of engagement and ton of view, the next thing is to start the 100k scaling step. You only need three steps to hit 100k. And those three steps you need are.

Note; make sure you give one or two week's interval. The first step should be first week followed by the second and third step

➢ Start remarketing your video view audiences
➢ Fanpage engagement audiences
➢ Lookalike audiences e.t.c

The kind of lookalike audiences you want to start building on the week three or more are

1. **Add to carts** – set of people that add your product to cart in your store.
2. **Engagement** – these are people that like, comment and share your post. You can also remarket to this group of people
3. **Video views** – with video view ads, you can remarket and retarget those people that watch your video
4. **View content** – you can also retarget to this set of people
5. **Purchases**

Out of this five section, the one you should really focus on is the video view, the video view is the one that will help you scale your ads to $100k.

Whether you are making $100 to $500 doesn't really matter. Once you are getting those **ROAS**, you can get started with this scaling strategy.

SCALING PLAN

Now that we know what is expected to know, open your facebook ads manager and click on *create audience.*

- ➤ Click on custom audience
- ➤ Click on engagement

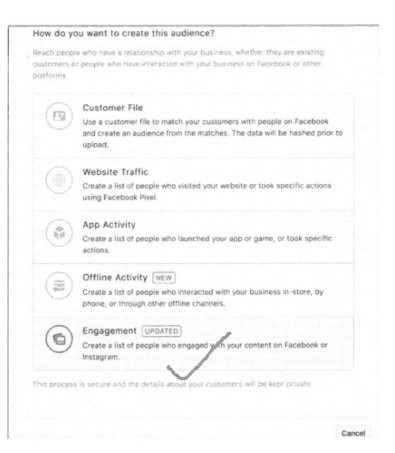

How do you want to create this audience?

Reach people who have a relationship with your business, whether they are existing customers or people who have interacted with your business on Facebook or other platforms.

Customer File
Use a customer file to match your customers with people on Facebook and create an audience from the matches. The data will be hashed prior to upload.

Website Traffic
Create a list of people who visited your website or took specific actions using Facebook Pixel.

App Activity
Create a list of people who launched your app or game, or took specific actions.

Offline Activity [NEW]
Create a list of people who interacted with your business in-store, by phone, or through other offline channels.

Engagement [UPDATED]
Create a list of people who engaged with your content on Facebook or Instagram.

This process is secure and the details about your customers will be kept private.

Cancel

On the next screen, you want to click **VIDEO**

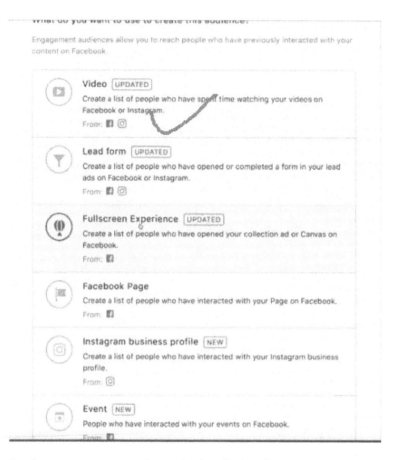

Engagement audiences allow you to reach people who have previously interacted with your content on Facebook.

Video [UPDATED]
Create a list of people who have spent time watching your videos on Facebook or Instagram.
From:

Lead form [UPDATED]
Create a list of people who have opened or completed a form in your lead ads on Facebook or Instagram.
From:

Fullscreen Experience [UPDATED]
Create a list of people who have opened your collection ad or Canvas on Facebook.
From:

Facebook Page
Create a list of people who have interacted with your Page on Facebook.
From:

Instagram business profile [NEW]
Create a list of people who have interacted with your Instagram business profile.
From:

Event [NEW]
People who have interacted with your events on Facebook.
From:

On the next page, you chose the kind of audience you want Facebook to retarget for you

Now you can see different category which is from 3% video view down to 95% video view. What this means is that there are a different set of people who only watch your video for a few minutes while some almost watch the entire video. If we are

Create a Custom Audience

Engagement 🟢	Choose a content type	Browse
	People who viewed at least 3 seconds of your video	
In the past 🟢	People who viewed at least 10 seconds of your video	
	People who have watched at 25% of your video	
Audience Name	People who have watched at 50% of your video	
	People who have watched at 75% of your video ✓	
	People who have watched at 95% of your video	

Back   Create Audie

to look at the profitable one here, I believe you will choose people that have watched your video for 95% but In this case, we are going to create a custom audience for the 75% video view. Later you can follow this step to create a custom audience for the 50% and 95% video view.

- ➢ Click the 75% video view.
- ➢ Follow by CHOSE CONTENT TYPE. Select your fan page and chose one of your video that is performing better
- ➢ Name your audience
- ➢ Add a description – about the ads e.g. best dog paw pillow from print on demand

Boom! By doing this you have automatically create 75% of people that have watched your video. One next step facebook want you to take is to create a lookalike audience on the next pop up screen

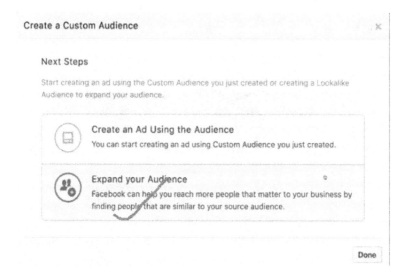

By clicking on the next section I mark with green, you will start creating lookalike audiences. What lookalike audiences does is that Facebook will immediately look for similar people who have similar interest for your ad and who have previously watch 75% of similar content to your ad on Facebook. Make sure you create from 1% to 10% to reach a large audience

Now you see there is power in creating a lookalike audience. Facebook will now build a total of 10 different audiences for you.

This is the only step that will make you scale to $100k fast. Note, don't forget to chose your location e.g. if you are selling worldwide chose worldwide as your location and if you are selling in a specific region chose that region. You can choose as many countries as you want but make sure is the area you can ship your product to.

Scroll down and click create and watch facebook performing the magic for you.

Once the audience is created you want to start with the 1% LLA. If profitable, do two percent and so on. You can spend literally $5+ per day for this kind of campaign

Don't forget this strategy should be done on week 3 or 4. On the following week, you want to start creating another audience, which is

> ➢ Facebook engagement audiences

Once you see the above step profitable, you want to follow the same step to create facebook engagement audiences.

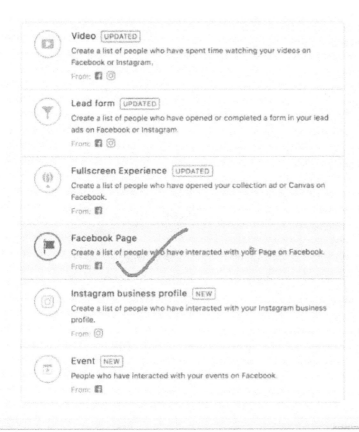

Video UPDATED
Create a list of people who have spent time watching your videos on Facebook or Instagram.
From: 📘 📷

Lead form UPDATED
Create a list of people who have opened or completed a form in your lead ads on Facebook or Instagram.
From: 📘 📷

Fullscreen Experience UPDATED
Create a list of people who have opened your collection ad or Canvas on Facebook.
From: 📘

Facebook Page
Create a list of people who have interacted with your Page on Facebook.
From: 📘

Instagram business profile NEW
Create a list of people who have interacted with your Instagram business profile.
From: 📷

Event NEW
People who have interacted with your events on Facebook.
From: 📘

This step is really awesome because Facebook gives you access to create audiences for any action your visitor perform on your page. See below for an example

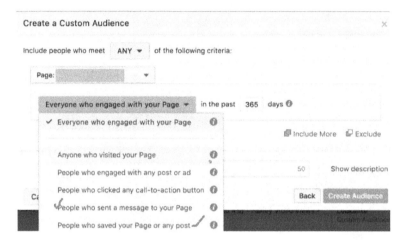

All this above are profitable but the most one is the one with the people that saved your page or any post. Name your audience and continue. On the next page, you want to click the section with FIND NEW PEOPLE SIMILAR TO YOUR EXISTING USER

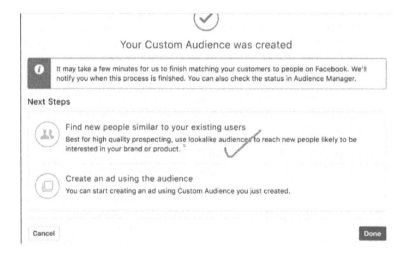

By doing so you will have another chance to create another lookalike audience. My man, there is a power in this strategy

and this will make you become a better marketer. After you are done with this, you want to build another audience for all the section.

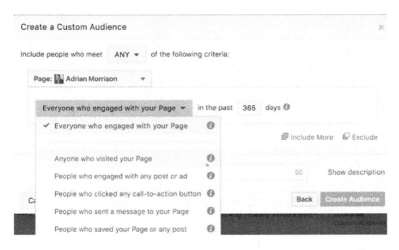

Wow, now you have learned a lot about scaling a campaign to $100k. All you need to do now is to implement this strategy to experience how it works.

CHAPTER 7. HOW TO GET PRODUCT REVIEW TO BOOST SALES

Social proof is another aspect you should take seriously when you start generates a lot of sales on your e-commerce store. getting social proof is not as easy as you think but with a layout (approved and proven) strategy you can get social proof as fast as possible if you start generating your first sales and have a happy (people who have received their product), customer. Put yourself in the customer shoes; assume you are looking for a product to purchase (either physical or digital) online and you find the same product on two different websites, one with product review (customer testimonial) and the other without no review. Though the two websites are legit and good to buy from, which of these two sites you will purchase from as a first time visitor (shopper?) of course I know you will purchase the one with customer review because they already have a happy customer who has already receive their product or find the service they offer valuable. Now I believe you know how important it is to have good customer review on your e-commerce site or any of your business website

TYPE OF CUSTOMER REVIEW

There are three type of customer review. Each of this customer review has their own different value.

- ➤ Text review
- ➤ Image review

- ➤ Video review

Out of the three customer review above, the most valuable one that converts better is the video review and it's very hard to get. All the review has its own value and they all convert well but the video an image review convert better and the text review happen to be the least converting testimonial out of the three but also convert well if you ask the customer to provide a deep review. Below, you will discover the right way to get customer review to improve your sales and improve your brand.

How to Get Review

To get customer review, you have to do two simple powerful step listed below.

Step one is

- ➤ Make a post on your facebook page or Instagram

Step two is

- ➤ Email your list to review your store

In the email and facebook post you make, you want to make your customer know that they will get something in return for reviewing your product and service

This strategy will help you achieve three main goals which are

- ➢ Build brand royalty
- ➢ Increase sales
- ➢ Trust and quality

This goal is exactly what we need to grow our store as fast as possible. Once we have this review at hand, we can do an undo and we can scale our Shopify store crazily and increase our revenue in a short period of time and keep scaling up till you create a trustworthy brand and have a very good royalty in the industry. If you want to build a strong brand always know that you need a customer testimonial to achieve that aim.

In other to get this kind of testimonial, you need to offer a very good decent offer for your customer. I mean an irresistible offer. And that is the kind of offer you can give to your customer to give you an awesome review. It should be a huge **discount or gift card**. Once you made such post e.g. giving away huge discount or gift card, you will see most of your customer come back to that post to comment something like "I got mine, I love mine, fast delivery, arrive without no dent, great customer service and so on" that will happen when you have a happy customer.

Another step you want to take when making that post on facebook, Instagram or either sending email broadcast to your list, you want to tell them what to do e.g. post your image, text, 20 or 30 seconds video of yourself with our product on your facebook page (you can either ask them to email the testimonial to you) or made the post on your product description but facebook fan page is always cool for this strategy.

HOW TO USE A CUSTOMER TESTIMONIAL

The main purpose of this testimonial is to increase conversion and increase brand loyalty. So once you receive this testimonial you can use them when doing

- ➢ Email marketing
- ➢ Sales page
- ➢ Product description
- ➢ Fan page
- ➢ Facebook ads

HOW TO MAKE CUSTOMER GIVE YOU REVIEW

To get a review, you want to either make a post on Facebook or send email to your list but the question is what kind of post should you post. Check out this example for the facebook post.

Customer Review or

Feedback Wanted!

Reward – 30% off Discount or Gift-card

Have you purchased a product from (brand name)? If so, we would love to get a review from you right here on this post

Just post a picture or video of yourself + the product in the comment below and we will reply to you with a

special VIP customer loyalty discount! The reason for this is we want to show the world to see how great our product and service is!

Got the idea? That's how simple your facebook post should look like. To make this stand out, you can add some cool emoji like money or fire emoji to make the post look attractive. Another thing you can do is to offer a higher discount for video review. You can do something like 15% off for text review, 25% or 30% for image review while video review should be 35% or 40%. That's just an idea.

Now when writing an email, you want it to look cool and very attractive by adding some image to make it beautiful. Don't forget to tell your customer where to do and where to make the post. Once done correctly this will make your **brand stand out** from other brand and also **generate repeat customer** for you.

Wow, this is all you need to know about how to generate a good customer review and you now know what most people in this field have no idea of. Go and try out this strategy and don't forget to reach out to me through my social network to tell me how this work for you

CHAPTER 8. ADVANCE FACEBOOK AUDIENCE TARGETING STRATEGY

You should really pay attention to this chapter because you are going to discover how to get your product in front of the people that are willing and ready to buy your product. The Facebook strategy that will be taught in this chapter is quite different from the one you have learned before and most people never taught this strategy for free, in fact, you need to join their paid program worth $1k+ before you will get access to this kind of strategy. By the ends of this chapter, you will be able to know how to take the data Shopify provided for you and use that data to get more targeted traffic from Facebook

HOW IT WORK

Think about it, you have a different shopper in your store; some buy an item worth $9.99, $10.99, $24.99, $49.99, $69.99 and $99.99 while some never spent a cent in your store. This is because all buyers (some will buy free + shipping product, some will buy a $5 flash sale product while some will a retail product from $20+ above product and some will never buy anything on your store) are not equal. The cool thing here is that Shopify keep this data for you but it left to you to know what to do with that data. Those people visiting your store are called prospect and customer. The idea behind this is, we are going to take each data (people who spent $10.99 or buy more than one product) on our Shopify store and provide that data to Facebook to find similar prospect or customer who is capable of spending that same amount of money on our store.

How cool is that!

This is an idea to make serious money on facebook. You are not only looking for customer to spend some certain amount of money on your store but with this strategy, you are looking for a qualify people who are ready to spend a lot of money on your store

Facebook have enough data to proof this. One thing for sure is that your facebook pixel cannot capture everything that is going in your store. Thanks to Shopify for providing and keeping every data for us that we can use for targeting similar interest on Facebook. Again this strategy has nothing to do with the Facebook pixel, even if you don't have facebook pixel installed on your store you can still perform this strategy but it's always advisable to have facebook pixel installed in your store.

With this strategy, we will be finding that different buyer e.g. people similar to those that have already spent $9.99, $10.99, $24.99 through to $99.99+ above on facebook. By providing that data to Facebook, we are telling Facebook to find people that will purchase a $10, $20+ product from us

IMPORTANT OF SHOPIFY WITH THIS STRATEGY

➤ Lifetime value (LTV) customer
➤ Done for you (DFY) audience

Note; whenever someone add a product to cart (ATC) or purchase a product from you, they automatically provide their personal detail to you and Shopify keep that data for you.

GETTING STARTED WITH SHOPIFY

Follow the step by step guide below to apply this strategy and grow your store fast.

Note, I will be using Shopify for this strategy. You can either create your Shopify store by getting my previous book (dropshipping goldmine) or check if the platform you are using stored this data for you. All you need is the data

➤ Goto Shopify dashboard
➤ Click on the customer tab

In the picture above, you can see the detail (blunt area) customer (name, address, email e.t.c) provided for us when ordering their product and you can see the amount of order and how much each customer has spent. Looking at the other area, we can find REPEAT CUSTOMER (customer purchases item greater than 1) and PROSPECT (customer who haven't buy anything – abandon cart) section (mark with blue)

You can also use the filter section to find customer value in your Shopify store. See the picture below

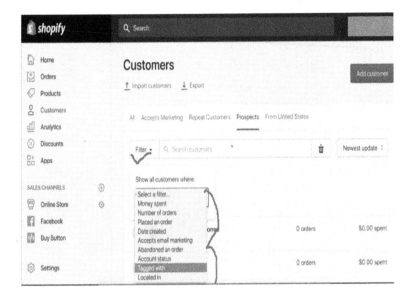

What you need to do next is to use the filter tab and select the

> Number of orders from the drop-down menu
> Greater Than
> Input 0 (zero)

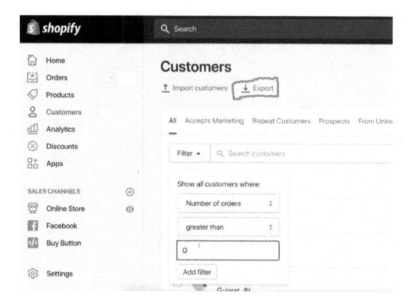

This will automatically look for people that have ordered one or more product from our store. What to do next to click the Add Filter and click on the EXPORT tab.

On the pop-up screen select the

> ➤ Select the 50+ matching search and
> ➤ Export as CSV for Excel e.t.c

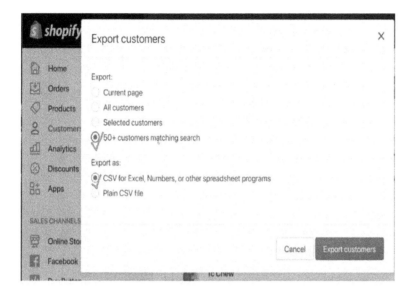

> Click on Export Customer

Once you hit the export customer tab, Shopify will email the spreadsheet to you via Email Address.

What happened here is that we will be getting the exact information customer give to us when checking out their product

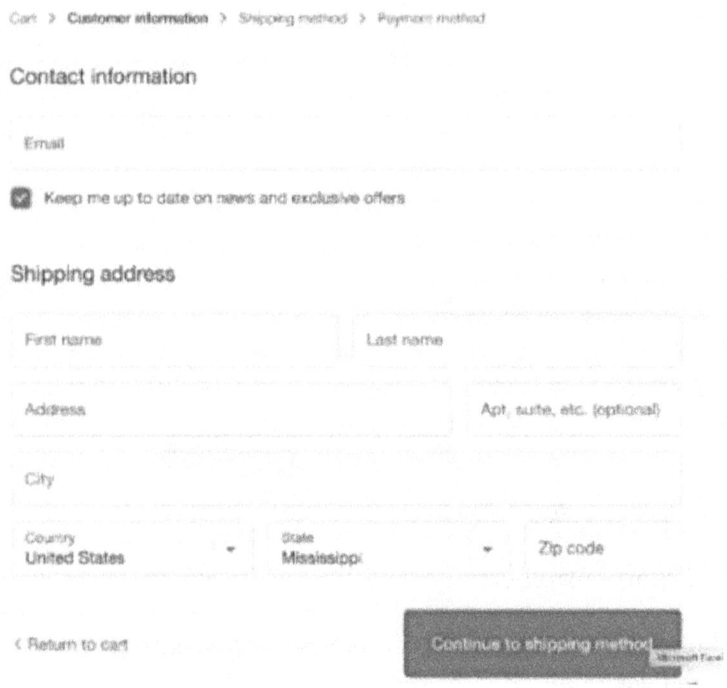

Cart > Customer information > Shipping method > Payment method
Contact information
Email
Keep me up to date on news and exclusive offers
Shipping address
First name
Last name
Address
Apt, suite, etc. (optional)
City
Country
United States
State
Mississippi
Zip code
< Return to cart
Continue to shipping method

See example above.

Once you receive the CSV file in your email the next thing is to upload that detail for facebook. See how the spreadsheet look like below

GETTING STARTED WITH FACEBOOK

Now, I believe you already have the CSV file sent to you by Shopify, the next thing expected to do is to give Facebook access to that file by uploading the data to facebook through facebook ad manager.

To get started with Facebook, login to your Facebook ad manager and click the

> ➢ Ads manager
> ➢ Follow by audiences

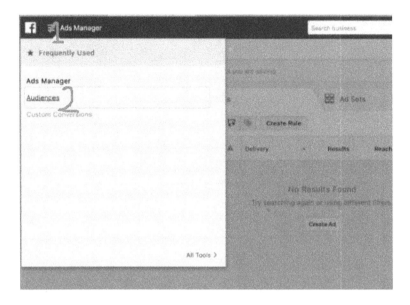

On the next tab, hit the create new audience. On the pop-up tab, click the CUSTOMER FILE.

We are doing something entirely different here and most marketers are not exposed to this method. What most people do is they use the WEBSITE TRAFFIC section and they create all kind of retargeting. Not that what they do is bad, they are absolutely doing the right thing but with this strategy, we going to upload the file Shopify provided for us and we will create our audience from it. Why this is important is that Facebook pixel cannot master everything happening in our store so that is why this strategy is important to those who fully understand Facebook marketing and how it works

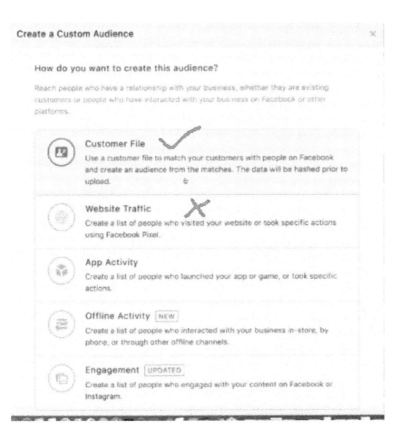

Read what Facebook had to say about CUSTOMER FILE to fully understand what this strategy is all about. What that means is that Facebook will help you create advanced audience to scale your campaign.

On the next page click the section I mark with green

Create a Custom Audience   x

Customer file

Add customers from your own file or copy and paste data
Use your customers' information to match them with people on Facebook.

Import from MailChimp
Import email addresses directly from this third-party connection by
providing your login credentials.

Customer file with lifetime value (LTV)

Include LTV for better performing lookalikes [NEW]
Use a file with LTV to create a lookalike more similar to your most valuable
customers.

Back

If you read the detail in the section I marked with green, you will discover that Facebook will create a LOOKALIKES audience for us. You can see clearly now that we will get the most valuable audience with this strategy because we are looking for people are ready to spend money on our store.

On the next screen, you want to click on the GET STARTED button and ACCEPT to import that file to facebook for the advanced targeting.

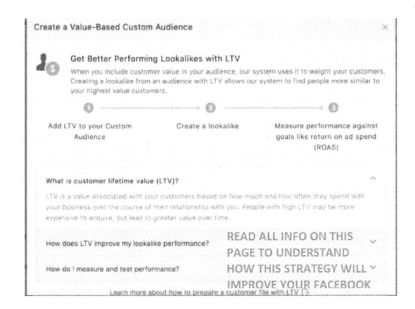

Create a Value-Based Custom Audience

Get Better Performing Lookalikes with LTV

When you include customer value in your audience, our system uses it to weight your customers. Creating a lookalike from an audience with LTV allows our system to find people more similar to your highest value customers.

Add LTV to your Custom Audience → Create a lookalike → Measure performance against goals like return on ad spend (ROAS)

What is customer lifetime value (LTV)?

LTV is a value associated with your customers based on how much and how often they spend with your business over the course of their relationship with you. People with high LTV may be more expensive to acquire, but lead to greater value over time.

How does LTV improve my lookalike performance?

How do I measure and test performance?

Learn more about how to prepare a customer file with LTV

Make sure you read all the information on this page to understand what you are about to do and learn how this strategy work. Another thing you need to take note is that this audience should perform better than all of your other lookalikes audiences. On the next screen, you want to name your audience, upload file and click next

Once you hit the next, it facebook will start searching the data you provided for them and they will ask you to chose the CUSTOMER VALUE you want them to access. Chose the TOTAL SPENT

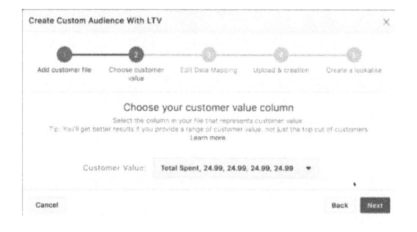

On the next page, you will be able to edit the detail you provided to Facebook. You can either submit the entire document or edit it to match your taste. Don't forget that the better data you provide for facebook equal to the better result you will get from Facebook. Just match up things an hit the UPLOAD AND CREATE BUTTON

Once uploaded, you will use this data to create a retargeting campaign. By getting this up on facebook, we just provided all the important data from our store to facebook to find the similar audience who are likely to spend that same amount of money on our store. On the next page, you want to click the CREATE LOOKALIKE button

Once we click the tab, we can now create a lookalike audience. From the file we submitted, Facebook will know who spent the most or less money on our store and who the repeat customers are.

On the next page, you want to create a lookalike audience.

You can either chose worldwide by typing worldwide in the location section or look at the file Shopify provided for you, check the best-converting country, type that country in the location area to target people in that specific region. In the audience size, do each percent that is from one to ten percent and click CREATE AUDIENCE.

This will strategy will allow your facebook pixel to fire fast and gather more info you can use later in the feature.

Now you know what most top facebook marketer or other marketer doesn't know. Go rock this strategy

Goodluck

ABOUT THE AUTHOR

DAVID NELSON is an Affiliate Marketer, Social Media Marketer, eBay and Shopify Dropshipper, Content Creation and Marketer, Email Marketer, Funnel Builder, Web Developer, SEO, and Business Consultant.

After studying the field above for four years, he decided to publish books on Kindle to help people who can't afford hundred and thousand dollar buy courses online.

David also loves educating and inspiring entrepreneurs to succeed and live the life of their dreams.

OTHER BOOKS BY DAVID NELSON

Dropshipping Goldmine
(https://www.amazon.com/dp/B07G2X1NSQ): Launch a
Profitable Dropshipping Business With This Simple Proven
Strategy

Instagram Marketing Playbook 101
(https://www.amazon.com/dp/B07K4B5S6H): A Proven
Step by Step Guide to Create and Grow Highly Engaged
Instagram page from Zero to thousands of Followers with no
Prior Instagram Experience and Make Money

UPCOMING BOOK

Advanced Facebook strategy – how to scale your Shopify
store or any business to $1k per day

Connect With Me

If you love to ask me any question, you can do so by following me on instagram.com(instagram.com/davidnelsonofficial/) , quora.com(instagram.com/davidnelsonofficial/) and reach out to me on facebook here(https://www.facebook.com/david.ecom.94) and here(https://www.facebook.com/david.okeke.399)

Connecting with me on this three platforms will be a great idea to reach out to me and know when I will be releasing another book that will help you make money online and live the lifestyle you wish

Leave A Review

If you enjoyed this book or found it useful I'd be very grateful if you'd post a short review on Amazon. Your support really does make a difference and I read all the reviews personally so I can get your feedback and make this book even better.

https://www.amazon.com/dp/B07J9MWK3Q

Thanks again for your support!

www.ingramcontent.com/pod-product-compliance
Lightning Source LLC
Chambersburg PA
CBHW070850070326
40690CB00009B/1775